Shakespeare for Students, Second Edition, Volume 3

Project Editor
Anne Marie Hacht

Rights Acquisition and Management
Lisa Kincade, Robbie McCord, Lista Person, Kelly Quin, and Andrew Specht

Manufacturing
Rita Wimberley

Imaging
Lezlie Light

Product Design
Pamela A. E. Galbreath and Jennifer Wahi

Vendor Administration
Civie Green

Product Manager
Meggin Condino

LIBRARY OF CONGRESS CATALOGING-IN-PUBLICATION DATA

Shakespeare for students: critical interpretations of Shakespeare's plays and poetry.-2nd ed. / Anne Marie Hacht, editor; foreword by Cynthia Burnstein.

p. cm.

Includes bibliographical references and index.

ISBN-13: 978-1-4144-1255-9 (set)
ISBN-10: 1-4144-1255-X (set)
ISBN-13: 978-1-4144-1256-6 (v. 1)
ISBN-10: 1-4144-1256-8 (v. 1)
[etc.]

1. Shakespeare, William, 1564–1616—Outlines, syllabi, *etc.* 2. Shakespeare, William, 1564–1616—Criticism and interpretation. 3. Shakespeare, William, 1564–1616—Examinations-Study guides. I. Hacht, Anne Marie.

PR2987.S47 2007

822.3'3—dc22 2007008901

ISBN-13

978-1-4144-1255-9 (set)
978-1-4144-1256-6 (vol. 1)
978-1-4144-1258-0 (vol. 2)
978-1-4144-1259-7 (vol. 3)

ISBN-10

1-1444-1255-X (set)
1-4144-1256-8 (vol. 1)
1-4144-1258-4 (vol. 2)
1-4144-1259-2 (vol. 3)

This title is also available as an e-book.
ISBN-13 978-1-4144-2937-3 (set) ISBN-10 1-4144-2937-1 (set)
Contact your Gale, an imprint of Cengage Learning sales representative for ordering information.

Printed in the United States of America

10 9 8 7 6 5 4 3 2 1

Twelfth Night

William Shakespeare

1601

Introduction

William Shakespeare wrote *Twelfth Night* possibly as early as 1599 but more likely in 1601. The earliest performance recorded is dated February 2, 1602, at the Middle Temple. Written most likely after the comedies *Much Ado about Nothing* and *As You Like It*, and before the great tragedies *Hamlet, Macbeth*, and *King Lear, Twelfth Night* has earned critical praise over the centuries for its superb construction and comedic form. Twentieth-century director and critic Harley Granville-Barker, for example, called *Twelfth Night* "the last play of Shakespeare's golden age."

Twelfth Night is most often praised by critics for its comedic structure and artistic unity. Its interrelated themes are complex and intriguing and have inspired many controversial and contradictory theories. Some view it as Shakespeare's farewell to comedy and note that its melancholy undertone foreshadow his great tragedies. However, most modern critics agree that festivity and Saturnalian pursuits lie at the heart of this play.

Twelfth Night explores a variety of themes and issues. The major theme of celebration and festivity was prevalent in all of the sources from which Shakespeare drew. The conflict between appearance and reality is brought to the fore by the elements of role-playing and disguise. Additionally, the use of language to deceive as well as the failure of characters to communicate effectively or truthfully are also issues studied and debated among critics and students of the play.

Act 1, Scene 1

Twelfth Night opens with Orsino, the Duke of Illyria. He is lovesick for Olivia and has been trying to court her. He has his musicians perform for him as he pines for Olivia. He surrenders to the way the music evokes emotions. When his attendant, Curio, suggests that getting out on a hunt might do him good, he responds that he would like to hunt Olivia. His attendant, Valentine, who has tried to get Orsino to face reality, arrives with the news that Olivia is discouraging suitors through her decision to mourn her brother's death for seven years. She will allow no one to see her during that time, let alone consider marrying anyone. Orsino is not discouraged by this news but instead expounds on how a woman with such a sensitive and loyal heart would be devoted to her lover.

Act 1, Scene 2

Meanwhile, a young noblewoman, Viola, lands on the shore of Illyria after a shipwreck, assuming her twin brother, Sebastian, has been lost at sea. The captain who saves her tells her that he spotted Sebastian trying to stay afloat in the storm by tying himself to a mast. Viola is conflicted about whether or not to hold onto hope for his survival. Regardless, she is now alone and needs a way to support herself. The captain, who was reared in Illyria, tells Viola about Orsino, upon which she recalls hearing of him and remembering that he had been a bachelor. The captain informs her that he is still unwed but that he is quite in love with Olivia. The captain explains to Viola about the death of Olivia's brother and her subsequent lengthy mourning period.

When Viola says that she would like to work for Olivia and be isolated from the rest of the world (so she, too, can mourn her brother), the captain tells her that because Olivia refuses to see anyone at all, she is not likely to interview and hire anyone new. Viola then determines to disguise herself as a eunuch named Cesario so she can work for Orsino. There, she will sing, play music, and curry the duke's favor. The captain agrees to help.

Act 1, Scene 3

At Olivia's house, her lady-in-waiting, Maria, admonishes Olivia's live-in uncle, Sir Toby, telling him that Olivia does not like his drinking and that she has heard that Sir Toby has brought a reckless friend, Sir Andrew Aguecheek, to court Olivia. Maria has heard that Sir Andrew is little more than a gambling, loud-mouthed drunkard. But Sir Toby insists that Sir Andrew is wealthy and well-educated, thus making him a good match for his niece. Sir Andrew, however, makes a bad first impression when he bungles Maria's name. When Maria leaves, Sir Andrew confesses that he does not think Olivia cares for him in the least and that it might be best if he left her to Orsino. Sir Toby dismisses such a claim, convincing Sir Andrew that he is a much better match for her; through flattery, he persuades Sir Andrew to stay.

Act 1, Scene 4

After only three days in Orsino's service, Viola/Cesario has won his confidence. When Viola/Cesario enters, Orsino sends the other attendants away so that the two of them may speak in confidence. Viola agrees to court Olivia for him, but secretly she wishes to be his wife. Although Viola attempts to convince Orsino that it is not a good time to romance Olivia, Orsino remarks that with as attractive a messenger as Viola/Cesario, Olivia is sure to pay attention. In fact, Orsino asks Viola/Cesario to carry on as if he admires her as much as Orsino himself does.

Act 1, Scene 5

Meanwhile, in Olivia's house, Maria and Feste, the jester, discuss Feste's recent, inexplicable absence. Maria warns Feste that Olivia is likely to fire him, but he still refuses to tell Maria where he has been. Olivia arrives with her steward, Malvolio, and when she tells the servants to throw Feste out, he uses his wit to lift her mood. Feste also asks Olivia about her mourning, and she explains that her brother has died. Feste tries to encourage her by reminding her that if he is in heaven, there is nothing to mourn. Malvolio challenges Olivia's decision to keep someone like Feste in her household, but Olivia defends her decision. When Viola/Cesario arrives to see Olivia, Malvolio attempts to send her away. Olivia, however, relents and receives Viola/Cesario after hearing how handsome and delicate he appears; Viola/Cesario, in turn, begins romancing Olivia by abandoning her rehearsed speech. Olivia is intrigued and sends her attendants away as Viola/Cesario eloquently delivers the heart of Orsino's message. But Olivia becomes more interested in the messenger than the message, asking Viola/Cesario about his upbringing and parentage. When she learns that he is of noble upbringing, she is impressed. Olivia ultimately sends Viola/Cesario back to Orsino with the message that she cannot love him, but also with an invitation for Viola/Cesario to visit again. To ensure Viola/Cesario's return, she sends Malvolio after her with a ring she claims Viola/Cesario left behind.

Act 2, Scene 1

On the coast, a man named Antonio has been housing Sebastian, the twin brother Viola thought she lost at sea. Although Sebastian had at first used a pseudonym with Antonio, now that he is well enough to move on, he tells his host his real name and the story of his sister. Sebastian tells Antonio that Viola has drowned in the sea, where Sebastian would have died too if Antonio had not saved him. Sebastian carries on about Viola's beauty and keen intellect, and wonders if it might have been better if he had died with her. Antonio decides it is best to leave Sebastian alone with his grief. Like Viola, Sebastian feels alone in the world and plans to travel aimlessly for awhile. Antonio has grown fond of Sebastian and wants to accompany him on his travels, but Sebastian is concerned that it might be too dangerous because of Antonio's enemies in Orsino's court. Sebastian leaves for Orsino's court, but Antonio stays behind because of the enemies he has there. Ultimately, however, he decides to risk the dangers of the court and follow his friend.

Act 2, Scene 2

Back at Olivia's house, Malvolio chases down Viola/Cesario with the ring Olivia sent. He is haughty and rebukes the young man for being so careless, telling him not to return on Orsino's behalf. Malvolio throws the ring at Viola's/Cesario's feet after she—playing along with the ruse—insists that Olivia keep it. Viola begins to realize the trouble her disguise has created. After Malvolio leaves, she picks up the ring and wonders if it signifies Olivia's love for Cesario. She feels pity for Olivia, who has no idea she has fallen in love with another woman. She says it would be better for Olivia to love a dream. In a matter of days, Viola has found herself in the middle of a strange love triangle.

Act 2, Scene 3

Meanwhile, Sir Toby and Sir Andrew have been up late drinking. Noisily singing and talking, they begin discussing logic and scholarly matters. It is an exercise in nonsense. Feste finds the two and joins in their drunken revelry. When Feste sings for the boisterous Sir Toby and Sir Andrew (who has been called to bring more wine), Maria warns them that they need to be more quiet or Olivia will have Malvolio throw them out of the house. Malvolio arrives to quiet them but is mocked by the merrymakers. He is outraged to hear such talk in Olivia's house, and he tries to shame Maria for taking part in the revelry. As Malvolio rushes off to tell Olivia what is happening, the trio plot revenge against him. Maria has the idea to exploit Malvolio's overblown ego by writing letters as if they were from Olivia; the letters will talk admiringly and lovingly about Malvolio so that he will believe his mistress is in love with him. The three are anxious to see Malvolio made a fool, and Sir Toby and Sir Andrew will eavesdrop to see Malvolio's response.

Act 2, Scene 4

The next day, Orsino talks about love to Viola/Cesario, revealing that he can tell that Viola/Cesario is in love. Viola/Cesario admits that Orsino is right and when pressed about the object of his affection, says that the one he loves is similar to Orsino. Clueless, Orsino encourages Viola/Cesario to give his affection to a younger woman who can keep a man's fickle heart for longer. Orsino then sends for Feste, who entertains at both Olivia's and Orsino's homes. After Feste sings a sad love song,

Orsino insists that Viola/Cesario go to Olivia again and tell her of Orsino's great love for her. Speaking again in veiled language, Viola/Cesario tries to convince Orsino that Olivia is no more interested in him than he would be in a woman he did not love. To make a point, Viola/Cesario tells a story about his father's daughter (whom Orsino assumes to be Cesario's sister), who was in love with a man but never told him, and died as a result. His passion for Olivia still alive, Orsino sends Viola/Cesario with a jewel to present on his visit to Olivia.

Act 2, Scene 5

Back in Olivia's garden, Maria, Sir Toby, Sir Andrew, and another servant, Fabian, are ready to launch their practical joke on Malvolio. Maria drops a letter where he will find it and runs away. The other three hide in the bushes to watch the action unfold. Surprisingly, Malvolio walks up and is musing aloud on what life would be like as Olivia's husband, the Count, enjoying all the power in the household. Just then, he finds the letter and identifies Olivia as the author. The letter is about her love for someone whose identity she cannot reveal, but it gives the following hint: MOAI. Malvolio concludes that it must be him because all the letters are in his name, after all. The letter goes on to say that Olivia wants to give power and status to her beloved. When he reads that Olivia wishes her secret love to confirm his love for her by appearing cross-gartered and in yellow stockings, being rude to Sir Toby and the servants, and smiling constantly, Malvolio assumes she is writing to him and plans to do everything she asks.

Malvolio exits, and the men come out of their hiding place. Sir Toby is delighted with Maria's work, and when she returns, they all laugh. They are particularly amused to learn that all of the things that Malvolio plans to do are things that Olivia hates.

Act 3, Scene 1

Viola/Cesario returns to Olivia's house as instructed by Orsino. He meets Feste outside the house, and the two enjoy some good-natured joking. Feste enters the house to announce Viola/Cesario's arrival. While he is waiting, Viola/Cesario soliloquizes on the nature of playing a fool and how complicated it actually is. Then he encounters Sir Toby and Sir Andrew, drunk as usual. Olivia comes into the garden and sends everyone else away so she can give Viola/Cesario her full attention. Olivia pleads with him not to bring any more messages from Orsino declaring his love. She boldly states that she is actually in love with Viola/Cesario. When he responds that he cannot love her or any other woman, he also tells her that he cannot return to her house. She begs him to come again, suggesting either that she thinks Viola/Cesario will change his mind or that she might be convinced to change her mind about Orsino. She is desperate for any excuse to see Viola/Cesario again.

Act 3, Scene 2

Lamenting that Olivia has shown greater favor to Viola/Cesario than to him, Sir Andrew decides it is time for him to go. Not wanting Sir Andrew to leave, Fabian and Sir Toby goad him into challenging Viola/Cesario to a duel to prove his love. They make him believe that Olivia may just be trying to make him jealous. Sir Andrew agrees to challenge the youth, and Sir Toby and Fabian volunteer to deliver the challenge. When Sir Andrew leaves to write the letter, Sir Toby and Fabian laugh at the joke they have arranged. Maria interrupts them with news of Malvolio having been seen wearing yellow stockings and cross-garters. He is making a complete fool of himself and does not know it. They rush off to see the spectacle.

Act 3, Scene 3

In Illyria, Antonio catches up with Sebastian, offering to accompany him for protection, and asks Sebastian to keep his money for him. The reader learns that the reason Antonio is not safe in Orsino's court is that there was a sea battle in which Antonio did significant damage to Orsino's forces. Sebastian agrees to travel with Antonio, who then goes to make arrangements for their stay at a nearby inn. They agree to meet in an hour, and Sebastian heads into town on his own.

Act 3, Scene 4

Meanwhile, Olivia sends a servant after Cesario in hopes that he will come back to her. As she waits and plans for how she will entertain him, she sends for Malvolio because she needs someone level-headed to help her devise a plan. When Olivia and Maria encounter Malvolio in his garb, smiling incessantly, and speaking nonsense (actually, quotes from the letter), Olivia thinks he has gone mad and sends for Sir Toby and Maria to attend to him. She has received word that Cesario has returned, and she is anxious to get to him. Despite Olivia's reaction, Malvolio still believes in the words of the letter. Sir Toby, Maria, and Fabian arrive to tend to him and pretend to be sure that he is possessed and determine to lock him in a dark room as treatment. Sir Toby takes advantage of the fact the Olivia thinks Malvolio has lost his mind and will not care what happens to him.

Sir Andrew arrives with a written challenge for Viola/Cesario. Sir Toby promises to deliver it, but instead he decides to deliver his own oral version of the challenge. He goes between the two, telling each that the other is enraged, violent, and terrifying. Neither really wants to fight the other at all, but they reluctantly begin to fight. Suddenly Antonio enters, and believing Viola/Cesario to be Sebastian, steps in to defend him. Antonio wants to fight in "Sebastian's" place but is recognized and arrested. When this happens, he asks Viola/Cesario for his money to pay bail, but Viola/Cesario does not know him. Antonio responds by calling Viola/Cesario ungrateful after Antonio saved his life, and she realizes as Antonio is being taken away that he has mistaken her for her twin, Sebastian, who must still be alive. Immediately, Viola/Cesario races off in search of her brother, much to the confusion of Sir Andrew and Sir Toby.

Act 4, Scene 1

Outside Olivia's house, Feste encounters Sebastian, thinking he is Viola/Cesario. Sebastian is understandably confused when Feste claims to know him and tries to get him to return to Olivia's house. Sir Toby and Sir Andrew arrive, and Sir Andrew immediately attacks Sebastian because he thinks he is the man who just fled the duel. Sir Andrew strikes Sebastian to continue the duel, but is surprised by Sebastian's skillful swordsmanship. Unlike Viola, Sebastian is not afraid to fight and begins hitting Sir Andrew with his dagger. Sir Andrew responds by weeping and begging for mercy. Feste threatens to inform Olivia that her new favorite is mistreating her uncle and her suitor. Sebastian has no idea what is going on around him and tries to leave, but Sir Toby stops him. After exchanging barbs with one another, they draw their weapons. Olivia approaches them, thinking that Sir Toby is about to fight the man she loves. She orders everyone away, apologizes to Sebastian for their behavior, and ushers him inside.

Act 4, Scene 2

Meanwhile, Maria and Sir Toby disguise Feste as a priest named Sir Topas to torment Malvolio, who is being kept in a dark room. "Sir Topas" speaks in a disguised voice and uses just enough Latin phrases and philosophical comments to sound convincing. Malvolio begs to be released and insists that he is perfectly sane, but "Sir Topas" pretends to misunderstand, and he lies to Malvolio about the room to try to convince him that he really is crazy. But Malvolio knows he is sane and asks "Sir Topas" to pose questions to prove it. In response, "Sir Topas" asks absurd questions and toys with the answers. When Feste returns to his cohorts, they all have a good laugh, but Sir Toby tires of the game. He is concerned that if Olivia finds out how cruel they were being to Malvolio, she will make him leave her house. He decides to end Malvolio's torment, and Feste returns to Malvolio, using his own voice and the one he used as Sir Topas so that it sounds as if they are having a conversation. Feste honors Malvolio's request for paper and pen so that he can write to Olivia.

Act 4, Scene 3

Although he is happy in Olivia's house, Sebastian wishes he could find Antonio to ask him advice. He comments that Antonio was not at the inn where they were supposed to meet. Olivia keeps giving him gifts and professing her love for him. He doesn't understand this rich and beautiful noblewoman's affection for him, and he keeps wondering if it is all a dream. Holding a pearl, however, gives him tangible proof that he is awake. He decides to go ahead and marry her when she shows up with a priest. They agree to have a more lavish ceremony later, as would be expected of someone of Olivia's social standing. But for now, they are content to wed in secret.

Act 5, Scene 1

Orsino and Viola/Cesario arrive in front of Olivia's house just as the duke's officers enter with Antonio. Viola/Cesario tells Orsino that it was Antonio who rescued him from the duel earlier. Orsino remembers him and asks why he came to a place he knew would be dangerous. Antonio tells the whole story of housing Sebastian and becoming close friends with him, only to have him betray him in Illyria. Angry, he accuses Viola/Cesario of abandoning him and keeping his money. Orsino dismisses it because Viola/Cesario has been in his service for three months.

Olivia then arrives and mistakes Viola/Cesario for Sebastian, her new husband. Orsino, thinking that Olivia has married his page, first wants to kill Olivia. He then decides to sacrifice his page, who willingly agrees to death if it would give the duke rest, and confesses her love for him. Believing herself betrayed, Olivia calls for the priest to attest to Viola/Cesario's pledge, who confirms it. Just as the duke decides to banish Viola/Cesario and Olivia, Sir Andrew bursts in, accusing Viola/Cesario of wounding him and Sir Toby. Viola/Cesario, however, insists that he was nowhere near the brawl. Sir Andrew and Sir Toby leave to find a doctor.

Media Adaptations

- Perhaps the earliest media adaptation of *Twelfth Night* was the 1910 film by Vitagraph. It was a silent film directed by Eugene Mullins and Charles Kent.

- The British Broadcasting Company (BBC) released a 1980 production as part of its "Shakespeare Plays" series (distributed by Ambrose Video Publishing) that continues to earn the respect of critics and viewers. It was directed by John Gorrie and starred Felicity Kendal as Viola, Michael Thomas as Sebastian, Sinead Cusack as Olivia, and Clive Arrindell as Duke Orsino.

- A 1996 film adapted and directed by Trevor Nunn and produced by Renaissance Films starred Helena Bonham Carter as Olivia, Ben Kingsley as Feste, and Imogen Stubbs as Viola. Nunn adapted the original to a setting in the eighteenth century.

Sebastian enters. He apologizes for his rough treatment of Sir Toby and Sir Andrew, and he is thrilled to see Antonio. As everyone looks at Viola/Cesario and Sebastian, the twins recognize each other. After a series of questions to confirm that they are each other's twin, Viola/Cesario asks Sebastian to wait while she changes back into her woman's attire. At that point, the onlookers understand that Cesario is actually a woman in disguise. Olivia realizes it is not Viola but Sebastian to whom she is married, and the duke gladly releases Olivia to him. Orsino realizes that Cesario is really a woman—Viola—who will gladly marry him. He recalls their conversations and understands that all along, Viola has told him that she loved him. Orsino is anxious to see Viola dressed as a woman, when suddenly everyone remembers Malvolio. Feste and Fabian earlier arrived with his letter, which is read aloud to the entire group. After hearing the contents of the letter, Olivia does not believe that he is insane and calls for him to be brought to her. When he is presented to her, he shows her the letter Maria wrote, and Olivia recognizes the handwriting. She quickly figures out the prank played on Malvolio and promises to grant justice to the wronged Malvolio, but he storms out vowing revenge. Fabian explains why the trick was played, and an announcement is made that Sir Toby has married Maria for her wit, as he suggested he might do earlier in the play. Orsino announces the upcoming double wedding (he and Viola will wed, along with Sebastian and Olivia), and Feste is the last one on the stage. He sings a song about growing old, and the play ends.

Sir Andrew Aguecheek

Sir Andrew is Sir Toby's friend. He is manipulated by Sir Toby to romantically pursue Olivia, and he finds himself opposing Viola/Cesario and later Sebastian in a duel for Olivia's favor. Sir Andrew is foolish and easily manipulated. It takes almost no convincing by Sir Toby to make him believe that an elite woman like Olivia would be interested in marrying him. Every time he tells Sir Toby he should leave because she is obviously not interested, Sir Toby tricks him into staying and continuing the pursuit.

Antonio

Antonio is a sea captain and a friend to Sebastian. He saves Sebastian from drowning and leads him to Illyria. There, he risks his own life to protect his friend.

Sir Toby Belch

Sir Toby is Olivia's uncle. He lives with Olivia and wants her to marry his friend and benefactor, Sir Andrew, in order to maintain a place in her household. Sir Toby is essentially a user; he uses Sir Andrew for his money and as a "straight man" for his jokes, and he also uses Olivia to have a place to stay. Sir Toby is highly intelligent, and even when drunk (which is most of the time), he can craft a pun and engage in spirited wordplay. He can also be cruel in pranks. He toys with Viola/Cesario and his supposed friend, Sir Andrew, when he riles them to fight with each other, even though neither one really wants to fight at all. He also takes an active role in the prank against Malvolio. And when he decides that the prank against Malvolio has gone far enough, it is not because his conscience directs him to stop, but because he is afraid his niece will be angry and turn him out of her house. Sir Toby and Maria serve as contrasts against the stark seriousness and ego of Malvolio.

Captain

The captain is Viola's friend. He saves Olivia from drowning and assists her in disguising herself as a pageboy.

Curio

Curio is one of the duke's attendants. He and Valentine assist Orsino by sending messages for him.

Fabian

Fabian is Olivia's servant. He joins the merrymakers Sir Toby, Sir Andrew, and Maria in the humiliation of Malvolio.

Feste

Feste is a clown. He is a servant to Olivia and entertains the residents of Illyria with his riddles and songs. He is the perpetrator of folly in the play and the polar opposite of his colleague Malvolio, Olivia's other servant. Feste's function in this society is to be an objective observer and commentator, and in so doing reveal the ridiculousness in the others' behavior. In his first appearance, in act 1, scene 5, he convinces Olivia that it is foolish to mourn her brother's death when his soul is in heaven. Later, in act 2, scene 4, Feste sings for Orsino, who requests a silly love song. Feste, however, perhaps to poke fun at Orsino's excessive lovesickness, performs a melodramatic song about a lover who died alone for an unrequited love. The duke in response briskly dismisses him. When Feste, dressed as Sir Topas, a priest, visits Malvolio in his confinement in act 4, scene 2, he tries to convince Malvolio that he is blind and that things are really quite different from the way Malvolio perceives them. In the final act, Feste summarizes the play with a song.

Commentators point out that, paradoxically, the character designated as a fool is the one who grasps the simple truths behind the action, which is that appearance does not always reflect reality. Feste observes of himself "*cucullus non facit monachum* [the cowl does not make the monk]: that's as much to say, as I wear not motley in my brain"—in other words, "the way I dress does not define me; while I may look stupid, my mind is quite sharp." When first encountering Feste in act 3, scene 1, Viola is one of the few characters to appreciate the depth of his insight when she observes, "This fellow is wise enough to play the fool, / And to do that well, craves a kind of wit."

Malvolio

Malvolio is Olivia's steward. He is tricked by Sir Toby, Sir Andrew, and Maria into believing that Olivia is in love with him. He appears in yellow stockings with crossed garters, believing she wants him to do so to prove his love for her.

Malvolio, whose name literally means "ill-wisher," first appears in act 1, scene 5, with his lady Olivia. His disposition is in direct opposition to Feste the clown, as Feste softens Olivia with his wit. Malvolio, however, is not won over. His insults to the clown prompt Olivia to declare "O, you are sick with self-love, Malvolio, and taste / with a distempered appetite."

Malvolio is the center of the subplot that develops in act 2, scene 3, as Feste, Sir Andrew, Sir Toby, and Maria are participating in revelry. Malvolio interrupts the merriment to say that if they cannot be quiet they will have to leave. The merrymakers mock and disregard Malvolio, so he vows to tell Olivia of the disruption their festivities are causing. In revenge, the four merrymakers devise a plan to make Malvolio look foolish in Olivia's eyes by capitalizing on his oversized ego.

In the fifth scene of act 2, Maria writes a letter

supposedly from Olivia and drops it in Malvolio's path. He is letting his mind wander to the preferential way Olivia treats him and contemplating himself in the role of her husband, the Count. Suddenly, he spies the letter and reads the cryptic message. His vanity identifies him as the object of Olivia's secret love, as he "crushes" the letters M.O.A.I. to fit his name. The letter asks its subject to appear smiling in yellow stockings and crossed garters, which Malvolio does at the first chance he gets to see Olivia, in act 3, scene 4. She thinks he has gone mad and sends for Sir Toby to look after him. The merrymakers torment Malvolio further in act 4, scene 2, by disguising Feste as a priest who convinces Malvolio that he has gone blind. Sir Toby finally decides to end the game, and Feste grants Malvolio's request for pen and paper, which Malvolio uses to record the injustices done to him for Olivia to read. When he finally gets an audience with her in the final act, she promises Malvolio that he will be both "plaintiff and the judge / Of thine own cause," but Malvolio storms out, declaring "I'll be reveng'd on the whole pack of you!"

Critics often note that the character of Malvolio stands in stark contrast to the atmosphere of gaiety that pervades the play. In a society where sensual indulgence is encouraged, Malvolio stands for law and order and is vilified for his position. He is fighting a losing battle. He has been compared by some scholars to the Puritans of Elizabethan times for his somber attitude and his crushing of the message in the letter to fit his fantasies, much like the Puritans bent the Biblical text to suit their own purposes. It is often noted that, because of his dissimilarity to the rest of the characters, Malvolio's presence in the play is critical. He plays the defender of the rules meant to be broken, in order to provide a scapegoat for the pranks of the merrymakers. Without the tension his character creates, the comic possibilities of the play would be severely diminished. Malvolio's punishment is particularly fitting because it exploits his own character defects. It is his own vanity that delivers him into the hands of the merrymakers and overcomes his rational restraint. Thus Malvolio is tricked into appearing to be the opposite of his true nature: the consummate killjoy is smiling and dressed like a clown.

Maria

Maria is Olivia's gentlewoman. She conceives and carries out the plan to humiliate Malvolio, and in the course of events she marries Sir Toby, who is her social superior. Maria respects her mistress and wants to help maintain order in the house, but she is enough of a rebel to be drawn into the plot against Malvolio. She is not a passive participant at all; it is she who devises the plan and writes the letter. With her wit and sense of biting humor, she catches Sir Toby's eye. She and Sir Toby serve as contrasts against the stark seriousness and ego of Malvolio.

Olivia

Olivia is a rich and beautiful countess. She rejects Orsino's romantic attention in favor of Cesario, whose twin brother, Sebastian, she marries, mistaking him for the pageboy she loves. She also handily rejects Sir Andrew's courtship, which she never takes seriously. Olivia is a highly emotional person who is initially seen throwing herself into the depths of a self-imposed seven-year mourning period for the death of her brother, and is later seen consumed with passion for Cesario. Olivia has little understanding of the needs and feelings of others and is content to have those in her court revolve around her every whim.

For all her faults, however, Olivia is not a flat character. Although her sentimentality is extreme, she does possess genuine feelings of compassion and pity. After all, she allows her uncle, Sir Toby, to live with her despite his not being a courteous house guest. She also pities Malvolio in the last scene when she reads his letter. She is able to ascertain that he has been the subject of a prank and not only calls for his release but assures him that the wrongs will be made right. Olivia also exhibits wisdom in running her household and managing her sometimes out-of-control servants and houseguests.

Duke Orsino

Orsino is the Duke of Illyria. He is lovesick for Olivia, and is trying to win her affections. Like Olivia, he is driven by his own unchecked emotions, and he lives in his own world of excess.

Characterized by melancholy, he pines painfully and longingly for Olivia at the beginning of the play but easily lets her go at the end when he discovers that Cesario is actually Viola, who is madly in love with him. He is prone to get caught up in his own emotional drama, which turns out to be very shallow. This is ironic in light of the speech he gives Cesario about how much deeper men's passions are than women's. In the end, he loves the one who admires him most.

For all his emotionalism and rashness, Orsino is also known as a gentleman who is brave and honorable. That he values honor is evident in his memory of Antonio; he is an enemy, but he does not discredit Antonio's honorable conduct in battle.

Priest

The priest is a holy man. He conducts the wedding ceremony of Olivia and Sebastian.

Sebastian

Sebastian is Viola's twin brother. The residents of Illyria assume he is Cesario, which leads to his betrothal to Olivia.

Valentine

Valentine is one of the duke's attendants. He and Curio assist Orsino by sending messages for him.

Viola

Viola is Sebastian's twin sister. She disguises herself as a pageboy named "Cesario" and courts Olivia on behalf of the duke. However, the plan backfires when Olivia falls for Cesario instead.

It is important to discuss the relationship between Viola and Olivia to better understand the characters. The principal scenes shared by Olivia and Viola begin with scene 5 in act 1, when the two women meet face to face. Viola has heard of Olivia from the captain and Orsino, but meets her for the first time when she arrives with Orsino's message. From early in the conversation, Viola/Cesario matches Olivia in wit and wins an audience with her, even though Olivia has heard Orsino's message before. Yet she is intrigued with Viola/Cesario's bold style and responds to Viola/Cesario's request to lift her veil. Viola/Cesario encourages Olivia to not leave her beauty in the grave but to embrace love while she is young and can have children. When Olivia starts asking questions of Viola/Cesario, it becomes clear that her energies have shifted from maintaining her refusal of Orsino to learning more about the page who is such an eloquent gentleman. When in act 2, scene 2, Viola/Cesario receives the ring from Malvolio that Olivia claims she left, Viola begins to realize the futility of the love triangle her disguise has created: "My master loves her dearly, *And I, poor monster, fond as much on him,* And she, mistaken, seems to dote on me: / What will become of this?"

Olivia continues to pursue Viola/Cesario, and Viola continues to deflect her attentions. When Olivia encounters Sebastian in act 4, scene 1, she asks him back to her house. When he seems amenable to her affections, she wastes no time in finding a priest to officiate the fledgling commitment between them. This, however, creates a problem when Olivia meets Viola/Cesario again in the final act, and Viola/Cesario acts surprised at Olivia's familiar tone. Viola confesses that she loves the duke, so Olivia, feeling betrayed and not wanting to be taken for a fool, brings out the priest to vouch for their vows. The confusion clears when Sebastian arrives on the scene, and Olivia realizes that she is indeed betrothed—to a real man. Viola is thus freed from her disguise and is engaged to marry the Duke.

The comparison of Viola and Olivia has engaged critics in frequent debate. Viola and Olivia, whose names are essentially anagrams of each other, are parallel characters in many ways; however, Viola is generally regarded as the principal character. The women begin the play in similar circumstances: Olivia disguises herself behind a veil of mourning, and Viola dresses as a pageboy. They both have also recently lost brothers. However, the women behave very differently. While Olivia chooses to waste her youth engaged in a meaningless ritual of mourning, languishing in exquisite self-denial, Viola continues to hope for her brother's welfare but chooses to get on with the business of living. Furthermore, it is Viola, some critics argue, who possesses the ability to see past the masks of the other characters, and who encourages Olivia to drop the veil and seize love while she is young. Olivia recognizes the value in this and does so, in a misdirected way at first, but with happy results in the end. Viola's arrival in Illyria is key to the action of *Twelfth Night*; without the insights she shares with Olivia and Orsino on love and life, the lovesick duke and the stubborn object of his affections may have otherwise simply grown old and died in a stalemate. Furthermore, Viola becomes interchangeable with Olivia to the duke, as he abruptly ends his pining for Olivia when he learns that Viola is a woman and he accepts her in place of Olivia as a wife.

Themes

Celebration and Festivity

Twelfth Night's light-hearted gaiety is fitting for a play named for the Epiphany, the last night in the twelve days of Christmas. While the Christian tradition celebrated January sixth as the Feast of the Magi, the celebrations of the Renaissance era were a time for plays, banquets, and disguises, when cultural roles were reversed and normal customs playfully subverted. The historical precedent to this celebration is the Roman Saturnalia, which took place during the winter solstice and included the practices of gift-giving and showing mock hostility to those authority figures normally associated with dampening celebration.

While the action of *Twelfth Night* occurs in the spring, and no mention of Epiphany is made, the joyful spirit of the play reflects the Saturnalian release and carnival pursuits generally associated with the holiday. The youthful lovers engage in courtship rituals, and the one figure who rebukes festivity, Malvolio, is mocked for his commitment to order. The Saturnalian tradition of disguise is also a major theme in *Twelfth Night*, with Viola donning the uniform of a pageboy, Olivia hiding behind a veil of mourning, Malvolio appearing in cross-gartered yellow stockings, and the wisest of all characters, Feste, in the costume of a clown.

However, some critics argue that, as Feste reminds the audience, nothing is as it seems; underneath the festival atmosphere of Illyria lies a darker side, which is revealed in brief episodes like the gulling of Malvolio. While the merrymakers contribute to the high comedy of the play through their practical joke, its conception lies in their desire for revenge.

Identity

Nearly every character in *Twelfth Night* adopts a role or otherwise disguises his or her identity. Viola disguises herself as a man upon her arrival in Illyria, setting the plot in motion. Feste disguises himself as a priest and visits the imprisoned Malvolio. The deliberate deception of these consciously adopted disguises provides a contrast to the subtle self-deception practiced by Olivia and Orsino: when the play opens Olivia is clinging to the role of grieving sister long after the time for such behavior has passed, while Orsino stubbornly hangs on to the role of persistent suitor despite Olivia's lack of interest in him. Yet another example of role playing can be seen in the duping of Malvolio, which involves outlining a role for him to play before Olivia—that of a secretly loved servant.

Critics have attempted to show how these disguises and adopted roles relate to the various themes of the play. Their overall effect is to make Illyria a place where appearances cannot be trusted, and the discrepancy between appearances and reality is a central issue in *Twelfth Night*. The roles and disguises influence the major characters' ability to find love and happiness.

Language and Communication

Wordplay is one of the most notable features of *Twelfth Night*. Feste's wittiness is an obvious example: words that seem to mean one thing are twisted around to mean another. He states that words cannot be trusted, yet he skillfully uses words for his own purposes. Viola, too, demonstrates a talent for wordplay in her conversations with Orsino, when she hints at her feelings for him, and with Olivia, when she makes veiled references to her disguise. In these instances, the listener must look beneath the surface meaning of the words being used to discover their true import. Thus, language contributes to the contrast of illusion and reality in the play.

Commentators have also examined how the written messages in *Twelfth Night* also contribute to the theme of language and communication. When the play begins, Orsino and Olivia are engaged in a continuing exchange of messages that state and restate stubbornly held positions that lack any real emotion to back them up. Another formal message, in the form of a letter, dupes Malvolio into believing that Olivia loves him. In these instances, formal messages convey no truth but instead serve only to perpetuate the fantasies of the characters in the play. Malvolio's message to Olivia is an exception: while he is imprisoned, Malvolio pleads his case passionately to her in a letter. This instance of true communication provides a contrast to the self-indulgent fantasizing of Olivia and Orsino.

Style

Irony

Because Viola has a dual identity, the opportunities for irony are rich. Viola, disguised as Cesario, is secretly in love with Orsino. When she talks to him, she hints at her feelings in a way that is very obvious to the audience (knowing she is a woman) but that eludes Orsino completely. She tells him that she is in love with someone very much like Orsino, and then she tells a story about her "father's daughter," who loved a man but died because she never told him. Of course, Orsino assumes Cesario is talking about his sister, not realizing that it is actually Viola talking about herself. When she tells that this sister died, Viola claims that now she represents all the daughters and sons of the house, which is true, but Orsino does not yet understand it. The irony is especially pointed because only Viola and the audience share the secret that reveals the irony. In the final scene, Orsino understands the ironic nature of their earlier conversations about love, and he immediately grasps the depth of Viola's love for him. His sudden emotional change at the end of the play is ironic, given the diatribe he delivered to Cesario about how much more deeply men love than women. In fact, his love for Olivia, despite all of his sighing and begging, is quite shallow. He is content to love the one who admires him and supports his ego.

Malvolio's attempts to signal Olivia that he returns her love are ironic. He is deceived into believing that she wants her beloved to wear yellow stockings with crossed garters and smile all the time. In reality, Olivia hates yellow and crossed garters, and because she is mourning her brother, she does not want to see those around her having silly smiles pasted across their faces. Every effort Malvolio makes to bring him closer to Olivia ironically pushes him away from her. To make this point especially clear, Shakespeare makes Malvolio's first appearance in this garb at a time when Olivia asks for him because she wants his help. She means to bring him near to her (though not romantically), but his ridiculous appearance and behavior provokes her to reject him completely.

Topics for Further Study

- Viola and Olivia are the central female characters in *Twelfth Night,* and their names are almost anagrams of one another. Create character sketches of these two characters in a side-by-side format that enables you to show their similarities and differences. What point or points do you think Shakespeare was trying to make with these two characters?

- *Twelfth Night* remains one of Shakespeare's most popular plays in production. Imagine that you have been chosen to direct the play, and the producers have given you complete creative control. What decisions would you make? How would you direct Viola and Sebastian to be convincing, yet distinguishable, in their alternate identities? Based on your perception of Malvolio, how would you direct your actor to make him more or less sympathetic? What would you look for in casting? Write out a plan for the producers, describing your vision and your approach.

- "If music be the food of love, play on," declares lovesick Orsino. Literature is replete with metaphors for love, this being just one. Locate three other metaphors for love in literature (drama, poetry, or fiction) and use them, along with Orsino's, to describe love to someone who has never been in love. You may act it out, write it in the form of a one-act play, or use any other presentation that is appropriate for your content.

- Gender bending accounts for confusion and humor in *Twelfth Night*. Can you think of a modern example of a play, movie, or television show that utilizes the same technique? Compare the two, with the goal being to conclude why this approach is universally entertaining, intriguing, and insightful. What is it about gender identity that is so basic to the human experience? Present a short lecture on your conclusions, giving examples to support your main ideas. Be sure to leave a short period of time for questions.

- If you had to choose one of the characters in *Twelfth Night* to love, who would it be? Which character is most appealing to you, and why? Write a love letter to this character, declaring your feelings in a way that would be best received by that particular character.

- There is nothing quite like acting out Shakespeare. Choose an acting partner and together, select a dialogue to memorize and perform. Do your selection for your class or for a beginning acting class. How does putting yourself *in* the play affect your understanding or appreciation of it?

- *Twelfth Night* has a second title, *What You Will*. What do you think this means, and would it be a better primary title for this play? Make your case in the form of a theater review in Shakespeare's time, as if you are trying to convince the bard himself that your point of view is correct.

- How would you characterize Illyria? Make a list of its qualities and those of its inhabitants. Is there a modern equivalent to this place? If so, what is it? If you are able to draw parallels between Illyria and a modern city, use photos of that city, quotes from *Twelfth Night*, and any other relevant selections to create a slideshow proving your point of view.

Hyperbole

Love in Illyria is accompanied by overblown speeches and exaggerated emotional expression.

Orsino is not simply in love with Olivia at the beginning of the play, he is obsessed with wallowing in his own sentimentality. He has his musicians play music for him that gives his feelings a rich context. Orsino is frequently swooning to music, love songs, and his own thoughts of Olivia. According to him, his extravagant love for her is equaled only by her cruelty at rejecting his passion. Even Viola indulges in hyperbole when she declares her love for Orsino in the final act. As she is ready to be taken off and killed, she remarks that she would willingly die "a thousand deaths" for him.

Grief finds hyperbole in *Twelfth Night*, too. Olivia announces that to mourn her brother will require seven years of hiding her face behind a black veil and seeing no one. Viola finds this approach to grieving so desirable that, upon arriving in Illyria and hearing about Olivia, she wishes to be in her service and join her in solitary mourning. Sebastian, too, takes his grief over the edge. He warns Antonio that he needs to be alone with the weight of his grief because he is afraid it will burden Antonio. As it turns out, Sebastian is so overly emotional with his expressions that Antonio (of all people) does not want to be near him at that time.

Historical Context

Twelfth Night

In Tudor England, a winter festival began on All Hallow's Eve (Halloween) and ended on the twelfth night after Christmas, or January 6. A Lord of Misrule was appointed to oversee the festival, and the Twelfth Night marked the end of his reign. Until then, his rule was characterized by the reversal of the normal order of things. This tradition of the Lord of Misrule traces back to the Roman festival of Saturnalia. Twelfth Night saw people feasting and taking down Christmas decorations. The king cake is traditionally served in France and England on the Twelfth Night to commemorate the journey of the Magi to visit the Christ child. In some Christian traditions, Christmas Day is the first of the Twelve Holy Days, ending on the Twelfth Night. This date, January 5, is the last night before Epiphany.

Textual Background

Twelfth Night was most likely informed by an Italian play titled *Gl'Ingannati*, (The Deceived Ones), which also utilizes themes of mistaken identity. Written in 1531, this play, in turn, informed the story "Apolonius and Silla" by Barnabe Riche, in his *Riche, His Farewell to the Military Profession*, (1581). The latter story supplied Shakespeare with additional plot elements missing from the Italian work. Matteo Bandello's 1554 *Novelle*, translated into French by Francois de Belleforest in his 1579 *Histoires tragiques*, is another version of this story. *Twelfth Night* also shares similarities with other plays within the Shakespeare canon: *The Comedy of Errors* also includes identical twins, and *The Two Gentlemen of Verona* includes a girl dressed as a page, who must woo another woman for the man she loves.

Reign of Queen Elizabeth

Queen Elizabeth is remembered as the great Tudor monarch who brought stability and growth to England over the course of her reign (1533–1603). The daughter of Henry VIII and Anne Boleyn, Elizabeth became what many deem England's greatest monarch. She was beloved by her people and respected among world leaders. During her rule, great artistic, literary, and naval figures ascended to prominence. Her efforts to strengthen England's naval power would have made her sympathize with Orsino and his vendetta against Antonio, who seriously damaged Orsino's fleet of ships at sea. It was during her reign that such events as the defeat of the Spanish Armada took place (1588). Her years on the throne were not without conflict, however. Europe was in the throes of religious turmoil, and Elizabeth's establishment of the Anglican Church, observing Protestantism, was controversial. Persecution against Catholics followed, with the religious question remaining far from resolved.

Elizabeth's court was widely regarded as a great cultural center. In fact, Elizabeth herself was sometimes the subject of artistic expression. Edmund Spenser dedicated his epic work, *The Faerie Queene*, to her, explaining in a letter to Sir John Walter Raleigh that his title character represents Elizabeth. She employed foreign painters in her court to do portraits, theatrical pieces, and other works. Elizabeth also patronized Thomas Tallis and William Byrd, arguably the greatest English composers of the time. She even set aside her religious intolerance for them; they were both Catholic, yet she extended her protection over them. Elizabeth was also a great lover of theater, and Shakespeare was a favorite.

Compare & Contrast

- **Late 1500s:** In Elizabethan theater, plays are performed exclusively by male actors, meaning that women's roles had to be played by men. Because of their youthful appearance, slight frames, and lack of facial hair, young men were cast in these roles. Audience members were accustomed to this substitution and thus had no problem accepting that men were acting as women. In some plays, however, where characters were hiding their true genders, the gender-swapping added a layer irony. In plays such as *Twelfth Night*, the fact that a male actor was playing a female character pretending to be a man added humor to the performance. In fact, playwrights sometimes went so far as to write lines that indirectly acknowledged this truth of Elizabethan theater.

Today: On the stage and screen, women play female roles and men play male roles. In cases where the actor's gender is different from the character's, the decision is made intentionally to make a statement, shock the audience, or play up comedic elements.

- **Late 1500s:** Twelfth Night is a popular and widespread celebration marked by masquerades, feasting, festivities, and traditions. People caroused in taverns, sliced up the Twelfth Night cake to see who would be that night's king or queen (one piece of cake had hidden in it a bean, coin, or small statue of baby Jesus), and drank wassail. In the seventeenth and eighteenth centuries, participants added actors and performers to the entertainment, and they often hosted elaborate balls.

Today: Twelfth Night is all but

forgotten, outside of the Christmas carol "The Twelve Days of Christmas." Even with the popularity of that carol, most people have no awareness of the traditional Twelfth Night celebration. In some Hispanic cultures, "King's Day" is still celebrated on January 6 to commemorate the Magi visiting the Christ child.

- **Late 1500s:** Ships are widely used for transporting people and goods across seas and oceans. Shipwrecks occur due to bad weather, faulty design or construction, unstable cargo, equipment failure, piracy, or navigational errors. Because maps are still being perfected, people who survive shipwrecks are often stranded with little idea where they are or how to get back. They also have little hope of being rescued.

  Today: Shipwrecks are very uncommon, thanks to advances in technology and shipbuilding. Ships are very safe, and the equipment used at sea helps them stay on course and avoid hitting icebergs, reefs, and other dangerous features. Further, when there is an incident, technology allows the captain to call for help. People generally travel across seas and ocean by plane, with the major exception of cruise ships used for leisure travel. Some industries, such as fishing, still rely heavily on ships (even in bad weather), but technology is available to keep the people aboard as safe as possible.

Critical Overview

With its hectic pace, intriguing characters, festivity, and trickery, *Twelfth Night* remains a favorite of audiences and critics alike. In fact, author and critic Harold Bloom writes in *Shakespeare: The Invention of the Human*, "I would have to admit that *Twelfth Night* is surely the greatest of all Shakespeare's pure comedies." Bloom finds that the structure of the play, although apparently spontaneous, is highly organized to reflect the craziness of the characters. He explains, "The play is decentered; there is almost no significant action, perhaps because nearly everyone behaves involuntarily." Much of the humor of the play arises from the characters's impulsive decisions regarding love.

The themes of celebration and festivity were central to the sources that inspired Shakespeare in writing this play. The incorporation of the Twelfth Night holiday was probably suggested by the Italian play *Gl'Ingannati*, which contained a reference to La Notte di Beffania, the Epiphany. However, recent criticism has reached past the surface gaiety suggested by the title and delved into the themes behind the temporary release of a celebration. Thad Jenkins Logan of *Studies in English Literature, 1500 to 1900* reveals darker undercurrents of the festivities of the play. He writes, "As its title suggests, the world of this play is a night world, and festivity here has lost its innocence." Logan reminds the reader that the celebration in the play appeals to pleasure and shaking off restraints, and he even characterizes the people of Illyria as "parasitical pleasure-seekers." He suggests that the message of the play is a cautionary one: "In *Twelfth Night* Shakespeare leads us to explore the possibility that our drives to pleasure are ultimately irreconcilable with social and moral norms of goodness." Within this world of revelry, there are two characters, Malvolio and Feste, who serve as counter-balances to the other characters's pursuits. Logan explains that as the play unfolds, the audience sees the need for the conscientiousness that Malvolio offers. He explains, "The play itself has discovered ... the dangers of life without the principle of order that Malvolio stands for—" As for Feste, Logan writes:

> There is within the play world one character who provides an ironic commentary on revelry, who seems to know that the pursuit of pleasure can be destructive, and who leads the audience toward a recognition of the emptiness of festive excess. Paradoxically, this is Feste the jester, whose name and office closely associate him with the festive experience.

Many critics have identified the problem of identity as a major issue in *Twelfth Night* and correlate the self-deception and disguises that are prevalent in the play with this theme. In an article for *Modern Language Quarterly* on the subject of identity problems in *Twelfth Night*, J. Dennis

Huston maintains that identity is an ongoing concern in Shakespeare's work and is manifest in Viola in this particular play. He writes that as she washes up on shore, "Behind her is the sea of lost identity, which has washed away the foundations of her previous existence. Gone is her childhood tie to family, for her father is dead, her mother never to be heard of, and her brother apparently drowned." Huston adds that Viola is separated from her hometown and must make her own way in the world. Her decisions lead to confusion about her own identity, and especially with her sexual identity, thus complicating her situation. But Viola must be appreciated as more than an angst-ridden young woman in search of her true self. Bloom finds her mysterious and enigmatic and remarks, "The largest puzzle of the charming Viola is her extraordinary passivity, which doubtless helps explain her falling in love with Orsino."

The use of language contributes to the sense of comedic festivity: much of the humor in the play centers on wordplay or choice of language. In *Shakespeare's Comedies: Explorations in Form*, Ralph Berry emphasizes the central role of communication in *Twelfth Night*, explaining, "The burden of the theme of fantasy and reality is entrusted to a particular device: the message. The action of *Twelfth Night* is in great part the business, literal and symbolic, of communication." He notes that the play begins with the message of Olivia's vow to mourn her brother for seven years. He lists other important messages, such as the false message from Olivia to Malvolio as well as Malvolio's letter.

Because almost all messages are misleading, Berry comments that "the comic business develops the serious concern of *Twelfth Night*, the fallibility of human communication." In an article for *Shakespeare Survey: An Annual Survey of Shakespearean Study and Production*, Elizabeth M. Yearling asserts that "often in *Twelfth Night* [Shakespeare] shows words to be frivolous, conventional, or false." She ultimately concludes, "Character and theme emerge from the nature of the words and the way they are combined." Yearling gives as examples words used "as mere decoration" by characters such as Sir Andrew, and "the language of compliment" that comes so naturally to the upper class, enabling them to seem polite when their intentions are altogether different. She pays special attention to Viola's way of speaking, noting, "Much of Viola's language, especially to Olivia, is affected, courtly, artificial, not the style we expect of a Shakespearian heroine. But Shakespeare exploits this conventional speech brilliantly."

Malvolio has intrigued critics for centuries. In the seventeenth century, Charles I was so taken by Malvolio's mistreatment that he changed the name of the play in the Second Folio to *Malvolio*. Critics in the nineteenth century argued whether Malvolio was a Puritan, or whether he represented the emerging bourgeoisie class, questions that are still being debated today. David Willbern of *Shakespeare Quarterly* describes Malvolio as a "humorless steward, sick of merrymakers and self-love, [who] seems almost a stranger to the festive world of Illyria…. Everything about Malvolio's character sets him apart from frivolity." Bloom interprets Malvolio as a stage version of Shakespeare's rival Ben Jonson. He elaborates, writing that Malvolio "is wickedly funny and is a sublime satire upon the moralizing Ben Jonson."

But there is a darker purpose in Malvolio's presence in the play. In the *University of Kansas City* Review, critic Melvin Seiden suggests that Malvolio's function in the play is as a scapegoat for the antics of the other characters. Seiden writes that Malvolio is in the play "so that Shakespeare's lovers may preserve their status free from the nothing-if-not-critical comic scrutiny which would otherwise expose their romantic pretensions to the withering winds of laughter." Seiden goes on to explain that Malvolio "is the scapegoat; he is the man who undergoes a sacrificial comic death so that they may live unscathed." Willbern acknowledges the gravity of Malvolio's sacrifice when he notes that the "underlying seriousness of Malvolio's fall is further suggested by the nature of the punishment he suffers…. Malvolio is not only mortified; metaphorically he is also mortally assaulted, killed, and buried." According to Seiden, Malvolio's role in the drama is absolutely critical to the success of the play. He maintains that "without Malvolio the comedy of *Twelfth Night* would be impoverished; I would go farther and argue that without him the comedy, the play as a whole, would not *work*." Willbern comments on the complexity of Malvolio's character as a man fundamentally divided. He notes, "Up to the moment of his fall, Malvolio had been able to keep his overt behavior and his covert desires neatly separate." Even at the end, Malvolio believes he is keeping up appearances, as Willbern explains, "But Malvolio's careful division between act and desire, reason and fantasy, collapses when he falls into Maria's trap, even though he himself is certain he has maintained it yet."

According to Bloom, "Malvolio is, with Feste, Shakespeare's great creation" in the play. Willbern goes so far as to call Malvolio and Feste "symbolic brothers." In fact, many critics pair these men as the two characters going against the current in Illyria. Feste is considered by many critics to be the best of Shakespeare's fools. Bloom applauds the character, declaring, "The genius of *Twelfth Night* is Feste, the most charming of all Shakespeare's fools, and the only sane character in a wild play." According to Alan S. Downer in *College English*, "Feste is disguised both in costume and in behavior…. His disguise, like Viola's, is a kind of protection; he is an allowed fool and may speak frankly what other men, in other disguises, must say only to themselves." Feste also plays an important role for the audience; Downer remarks that Feste's function is "to make plain to the audience the artificial, foolish attitudes of the principal figures." Commenting on Feste's pivotal role in the play, Downer points to the moment when Feste drives Sebastian and Olivia together. He writes, "It is Feste's only direct contribution to the action of the play; it is also the single decisive action which cuts the comic knot; and it is a visual dramatic symbol of his relationship to the whole play." *ELH*'s Joan Hartwig adds another dimension of meaning in interpreting Feste's function in the play. According to Hartwig:

> Feste's manipulation of Malvolio resembles the playwright's manipulation of his audience's will, but in such a reduced way that we cannot avoid seeing the difference between merely human revenge and the larger benevolence that control's the play's design.

What Do I Read Next?

- Anthony Holden's 2002 *William Shakespeare: An Illustrated Biography* offers readers an honest attempt to present the facts of Shakespeare's life, separate from the legends that surround the playwright. The book is brought to life by the inclusion of illustrations and ephemera related to the bard's life.

- In *Shakespeare's Comedy of Love* (1974), Alexander Legatt offers an extended analysis of the play, concluding that *Twelfth Night* is unique among Shakespeare's comedies in its depiction of the opposition between an ideal "golden world" of order and the seemingly disordered everyday world.

- *As You Like It* is among Shakespeare's most popular comedies. Written in approximately 1599, the play explores themes of comedy, social expectations, and power. In addition to their affection for the heroine, Rosalind, audience members are intrigued by elements of gender confusion, trickery, and true love.

- Written for actors, producers, and directors, Michael Pennington's *Twelfth Night: A User's Guide* (2004) presents a solid understanding of the play, along with practical considerations for performing it on today's stage.

- Edited by Bruce R. Smith, *Twelfth Night: Texts and Contexts* (2001) contains a wide range of historical and cultural documents shedding light on such topics as Puritan conduct, household economy, the history of *Twelfth Night*'s production, and boy actors in Elizabethan drama.

- The Teaching Shakespeare Institute's *Shakespeare Set Free: Teaching Twelfth Night and Othello* (2006) is a resource for teachers and serious students, complete with in-depth essays, assignment ideas, and performance techniques.

Sources

Berry, Ralph, "The Messages of *Twelfth Night*," in *Shakespeare's Comedies: Explorations in Form*, Princeton University Press, 1972, pp. 196-212.

Bloom, Harold, "Twelfth Night," in *Shakespeare: The Invention of the Human*, Riverhead Books, 1998, pp. 226-46.

Downer, Alan S., "Feste's Night," in *College English*, Vol. 13, No. 5, February 1952, pp. 258-65.

Granville-Barker, Harley, "Preface to *Twelfth Night*," in *Prefaces to Shakespeare, Vol. 6*, B. T. Batsford Ltd., 1974, pp. 26-32.

Hartwig, Joan, "Feste's 'Whirligig of Time' and the Comic Providence of *Twelfth Night*," in *ELH*, Vol. 40, No. 4, Winter 1973, pp. 501-13.

Huston, J. Dennis, "When I Came to Man's Estate: *Twelfth Night* and Problems of Identity," in *Modern Language Quarterly*, Vol. 33, No. 3, September 1972, pp. 274-88.

Logan, Thad Jenkins, "*Twelfth Night*: The Limits of Festivity," in *Studies in English Literature, 1500 to 1900*, Vol. 22, No. 2, Spring 1982, pp. 223-38.

Seiden, Melvin, "Malvolio Reconsidered," in *University of Kansas City Review*, Vol. 28, No. 2, December 1961, pp. 105-14.

Shakespeare, William, *Twelfth Night*, 2nd Series, edited by J. M. Lothian and T. W. Craik, Arden

Shakespeare, 1975.

Willbern, David, "Malvolio's Fall," in *Shakespeare Quarterly*, Vol. 29, No. 1, Winter 1978, pp. 85-90.

Yearling, Elizabeth M., "Language, Theme, and Character in *Twelfth Night*," in *Shakespeare Survey: An Annual Survey of Shakespearean Study and Production*, Vol. 35, 1982, pp. 79-86.

Further Reading

Berry, Ralph, "The Season of *Twelfth Night,*" *New York Literary Forum*, Vol. 1, Spring 1978, pp. 139-49.

> Berry compares late nineteenth-century productions of the play with modern ones, finding that the former emphasized comedic elements of the play at the expense of its darker themes.

—————, "'Twelfth Night': The Experience of the Audience," in *Shakespeare Survey*, Vol. 34, 1981, pp. 111-19.

> Berry contends that the play would have had a disturbing effect on its original audiences, much like a joke that goes too far.

Crane, Milton, "*Twelfth Night* and Shakespearean Comedy," in *Shakespeare Quarterly*, Vol. 6, No. 1, Winter 1955, pp. 1-8.

> Crane places *Twelfth Night* in the context of Shakespeare's comedies, which Crane contends are based upon themes of classical comedy but depart from these conventions to an increasingly larger degree in the later plays.

Donno, Elizabeth Story, "Introduction" to *Twelfth*

Night or *What You Will*, by William Shakespeare, Cambridge University Press, 1985, pp. 1-40.

> Donno provides an overview of issues relating to the play, including its sources, theatrical history, and critical commentary.

Eagleton, Terrence, "Language and Reality in 'Twelfth Night,'" in *The Critical Quarterly*, Vol. 9, No. 3, Autumn 1967, pp. 217-28.

> Eagleton delves into the complex relationship between language, roles, and illusion in the play.

Fleming, William H., "*Twelfth Night*," in *Shakespeare' Plots: A Study in Dramatic Construction*, Hutchinson & Co., 1949, pp. 68-76.

> Fleming praises the lyrical elements of *Twelfth Night* as a means of expressing the theme of love, and discusses the humor, farce, and satire within the play.

Fortin, René E., "*Twelfth Night*: Shakespeare's Drama of Initiation," in *Papers on Language and Literature*, Vol. 8, No. 2, Spring 1972, pp. 135-46.

> Fortin provides a symbolic interpretation of the play as a drama centering on Viola's search for her sexual identity.

Gaskill, Gayle, "The Role of Fortune in *Twelfth Night*," in *Iowa English Bulletin*, Vol. 30, No. 1, Fall 1980, pp. 20-23, 32.

Gaskill examines the workings of fortune in the play and how each character's nature is revealed by their reaction to it.

Gerard, Albert, "Shipload of Fools: A Note on *Twelfth Night*," in *English Studies*, Vol. 45, No. 2, Autumn 1964, p. 109.

Gerard demonstrates that in *Twelfth Night*, there are intimations of the tragic themes of Shakespeare's later plays.

Lewalski, Barbara K., "Thematic Patterns in *Twelfth Night*," in *Shakespeare Studies: An Annual Gathering of Research, Criticism, and Reviews*, Vol. 1, 1965, pp. 168-81.

Lewalski discusses the pagan celebration of Twelfth Night and examines the Christian concept of Epiphany in the play.

Siegel, Paul N., "Malvolio: Comic Puritan Automaton," in *New York Literary Forum*, Vol. 6, 1980, pp. 217-30.

Siegel analyzes Malvolio as a representation of Puritan self-discipline and predictability.

Stane, Bob, "The Genealogy of Sir Andrew Aguecheek," in *The Shakespeare Newsletter*, Vol. 32, Nos. 5-6, Winter 1982, p. 32.

Stane suggests that the role of Sir Andrew Aguecheek was inspired by a personality type readily recognizable to all levels of English society.

Swander, Homer, "*Twelfth Night*: Critics, Players, and a Script," in *Educational Theatre Journal*, Vol. 16, No. 2, May 1964, pp. 114-21.

This article surveys critical reactions to various New York productions of the play, arguing that to be successful a production must convey the underlying moral warning against self-love and folly.

Williams, Porter, Jr., "Mistakes in *Twelfth Night* and Their Resolution: A Study in Some Relationships of Plot and Theme," in *PMLA*, Vol. 76, No. 3, June 1961, 193-99.

Williams shows how the mistakes made by characters in the play reveal themes of love and personal relationships common to all of Shakespeare's comedies.

Lightning Source UK Ltd.
Milton Keynes UK
UKHW020427130121
376916UK00011B/2374